Changing Shores

By Pamela Jennett

CELEBRATION PRESS
Pearson Learning Group

Contents

Where Land Meets Water

Earth appears to be a small, blue planet when it is seen from outer space. It looks blue because it is mostly made up of water. Some of the landmasses can be seen from space.

Most of Earth's surface is covered by water.

Each landmass is shaped differently.
All landmasses have **shores** where the land
meets the ocean or sea. This is called the shoreline
or coastline.

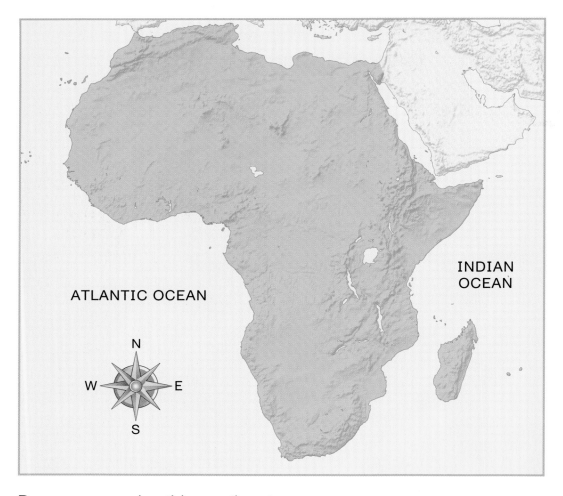

Do you recognize this continent
by its shape? This is Africa.

On most continents there are a number
of countries. Some of the countries have
a shoreline and others do not.

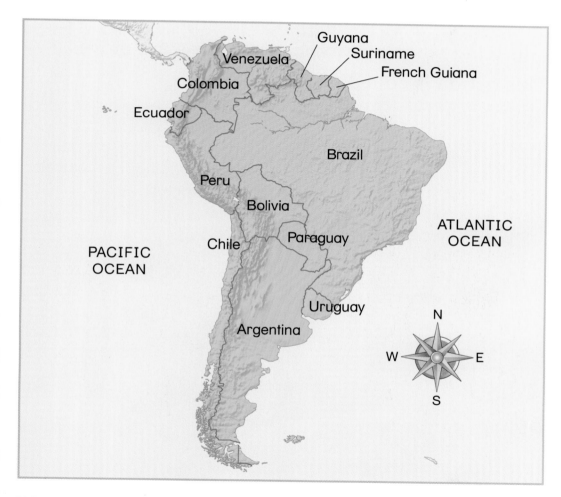

Which two countries in South America
do not have shorelines?

How Shores Change

Like the Earth itself, the shores change all of the time. The wind and the waves of the ocean pound against the land. Water and wind wear away the rock. The sand moves. This action is called **erosion**.

Constant pounding from waves erodes the rocks.

Sometimes erosion causes a sandy beach to form over time. This happens when waves pick up rocks, pebbles, and other materials from the shore. The motion of the waves grinds these things together. Then they break apart into small pieces.

Some shorelines are made up of only sand.
Sandy shorelines change shape all of the time.
The sand may shift in all directions.

The patterns on this beach show how
the sand has shifted.

sand spit

As the sand shifts, it sometimes builds up along the shoreline. A **sand spit** may form if the sand connects to the shore. If wind blows sand high up on to the shore, it may form a **sand dune**.

a sand dune

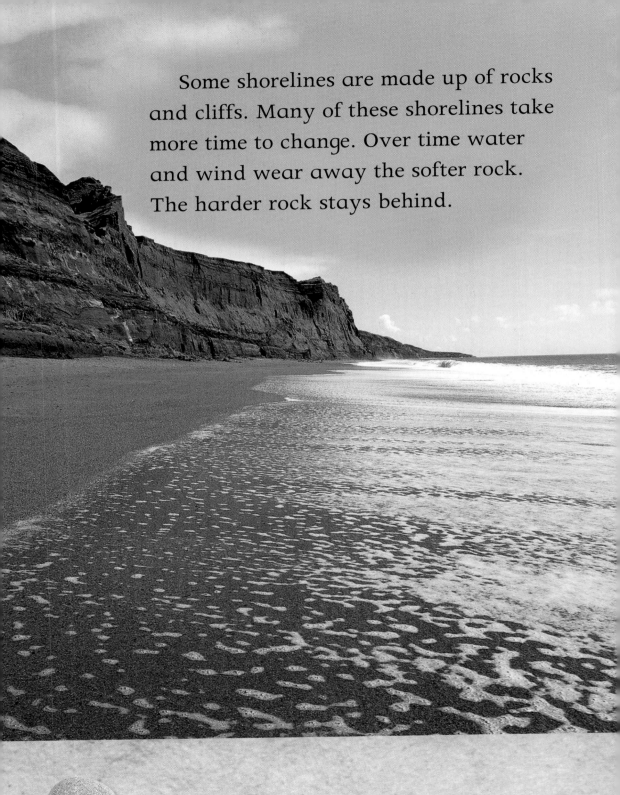

Some shorelines are made up of rocks and cliffs. Many of these shorelines take more time to change. Over time water and wind wear away the softer rock. The harder rock stays behind.

arch

rock stack

Rough waves can cut into rock and form caves and **arches**. After a long time some arches collapse. A **rock stack** may be left behind.

A Changing Shore in Great Britain

Most changes to the shores take hundreds or thousands of years. However, sometimes change happens quickly. A shoreline can even change overnight.

The Holderness Coast is the fastest eroding shoreline in Europe.

N

Great Britain

The Holderness Coast in Great Britain is a shoreline that changes all of the time. Every year about 6 feet of shoreline erodes into the sea. During the last 2,000 years the shore has **receded** almost 1,300 feet.

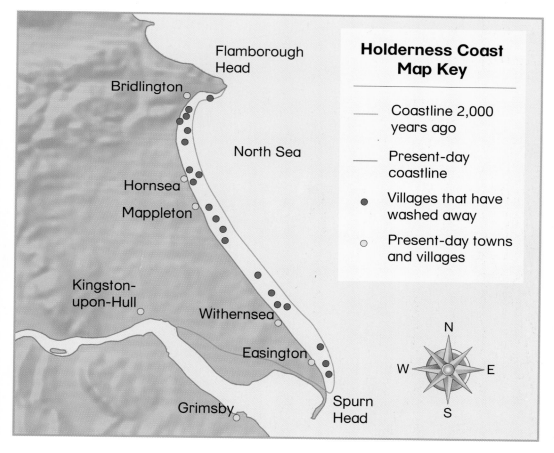

Flamborough Head

Bridlington

North Sea

Hornsea

Mappleton

Kingston-upon-Hull

Withernsea

Easington

Grimsby

Spurn Head

Holderness Coast Map Key

―――― Coastline 2,000 years ago

―――― Present-day coastline

● Villages that have washed away

○ Present-day towns and villages

N
W ＋ E
S

Many villages along the Holderness Coast have been washed into the sea.

Along the Holderness Coast the cliffs are
very soft. The rock cracks easily and breaks away.
The cliffs slide into the water. The rock is washed
away by rough storm waves.

Caves form in the soft rock.

Stop

People live and work on the cliffs above the shore. When the cliffs break away, the streets are destroyed. People's homes and other buildings sometimes fall into the sea.

Often people see the coastline change.

At one time Owthorne Church stood
at the edge of the cliff. The cliffs kept
breaking away, and the shore kept receding.
Now the church is under the North Sea.

The Holderness Coast continues to change every day. As the waves erode the land, the shoreline will change. People still live near the coast, though. They try to protect their homes from the constant erosion.

People build walls to help protect the coastline and their homes.

The Power of Storms

Hurricanes can change shores quickly. Hurricanes are also called **cyclones**. These storms start over warm, tropical oceans. When a hurricane moves over the shore and onto the land, it can be very dangerous. The pounding rain, strong winds, and huge waves affect the land.

In 1992 Hurricane Andrew hit the United States. The storm moved across Florida and along the Gulf Coast. It was one of the worst hurricanes to ever strike that area.

Hurricane Andrew

This satellite photograph shows the size of Hurricane Andrew.

On August 26, 1992, Hurricane Andrew passed over the many islands off the coast of Louisiana. The storm pounded the small islands. The wind, rain, and waves changed the shores of many of them.

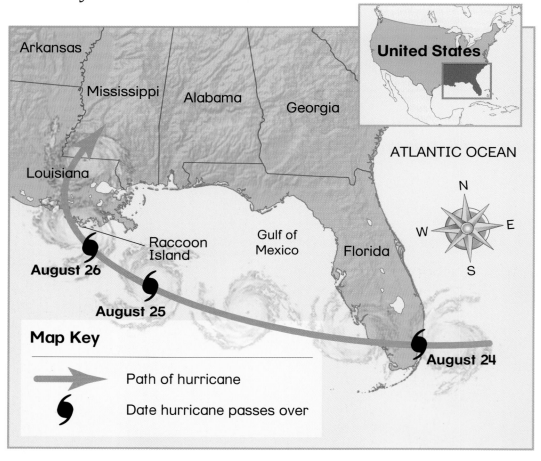

Hurricane Andrew moved from the Atlantic Ocean to the Gulf of Mexico.

One of the islands affected was Raccoon Island. The beach on Raccoon Island was washed away during the hurricane. The shoreline of the island was changed almost overnight.

Before Hurricane Andrew

After Hurricane Andrew

Forever Changing

The Earth's shorelines are constantly changing. Usually the changes are slow. Sometimes the changes are quick. These changes make each shore different.

Glossary

arches   curved structures that go across an open space

cyclones   tropical storms with very strong winds and heavy rain

hurricanes   large storms with strong winds and heavy rain

erosion   the process of wearing away by water or wind

receded   moved back or away from

rock stack   part of rock left behind after an arch collapses

sand dune   a mound or ridge of sand built up on the shore

sand spit   a narrow point of land that extends into a body of water

shores   land along the edge of bodies of water

Index